THE NEED TO KNOW LIBRARY™

EVERYTHING YOU NEED TO KNOW ABOUT

PROTESTS AND PUBLIC ASSEMBLY

PHILIP WOLNY

Rosen
YA™

New York

Published in 2019 by The Rosen Publishing Group, Inc.
29 East 21st Street, New York, NY 10010

Copyright © 2019 by The Rosen Publishing Group, Inc.

First Edition

Cataloging-in-Publication Data

Names: Wolny, Philip, author.
Title: Everything you need to know about protests and public assembly / Philip Wolny.
Description: New York : Rosen Publishing, 2019. | Series: The need to know library | Includes bibliographical references and index. | Audience: Grades 7–12.
Identifiers: ISBN 9781508179207 (library bound) | ISBN 9781508179290 (pbk.)
Subjects: LCSH: Assembly, Right of—United States—Juvenile literature. | Freedom of speech—United States—Juvenile literature. | Demonstrations—United States—Juvenile literature. | Protest movements—United States—Juvenile literature.
Classification: LCC KF4778.W65 2019 | DDC 342.7308'54—dc23

Manufactured in the United States of America

On the cover: This protest against a speech by Maine state representative Lawrence Lockman took place on February 16, 2017. The protesters argued that Lockman was racist and xenophobic.

CONTENTS

INTRODUCTION

In the summer of 2017, two groups of activists faced off in Charlottesville, Virginia. A gathering of white supremacist and white nationalist groups staged infamous rallies in Charlottesville, Virginia, that made news around the world. The organizers—under the umbrella name Unite the Right—said they were protesting the city council's upcoming removal of a statue of Robert E. Lee from a park. They also claimed to be marching to demand and demonstrate their right of free speech.

Counterprotesters—many of them student activists, including socialists and those active with the Black Lives Matter (BLM) movement against police violence—challenged the far right marchers on the streets. Nonviolent clergy and others tried to block the often aggressive marchers from entering Emancipation Park, where the protest was to take place. Others on the side of the counterprotesters included the black-clad Antifascists, or Antifa for short. Many people credited them with physically protecting them from attacks from the far-right contingent. Meanwhile, police had done little to separate the parties involved. Violence broke out everywhere. The worst came when a thirty-two-year-old socialist, activist, and paralegal named Heather Heyer was run down and killed by a white supremacist named James Alex Fields Jr.

White nationalist activists under the "Unite the Right" umbrella (*left*) physically grappled with antifascist and other counterprotesters in the streets of Charlottesville, Virginia, on August 12, 2017.

The weekend and its aftermath came at a tense time in American politics and society. Protest movements against globalization in the 1990s and 2000s, as well as the Occupy movement and BLM, among other social justice campaigns, have motivated many to take to the streets for rallies, marches, and other actions. It has not only been people on the left side of the political spectrum that have become motivated. Conservative Americans have shown up for protests organized by the Tea Party movement in opposition to President Barack Obama and some of his policies. Far-right groups that are nationalist, anti-immigrant, and anti-Muslim, have been on the march, too.

Things may seem messy and chaotic, even frightening. But many periods of American history and change have been marked by protest. The right to protest against one's government or other parties, and to peaceably assemble, is one of the most important ones for the health of our society and legal system. Many of today's young people, including students now in high school or college, have stepped up in the past few years to make themselves heard. Knowing more about their rights, the limits to those rights, and how to defend those rights is crucial for them to be responsible and engaged citizens. In a time when the political landscape can seem uncertain, knowledge is power. That power will translate to teens feeling confident in themselves, expressing their views, and fighting for the things they believe in a safe and nonviolent fashion.

CHAPTER ONE

A LEGACY OF PROTEST

The rights of protest and public assembly have been crucial in US history. Protests, demonstrations, and other forms of activism played a role in the American Revolution, without which the United States would not be a country. Protest has also brought about many of the social changes that followed and continues to be one of the most powerful forces of change.

FOUNDING PRINCIPLES

By the time of the American Revolution, tensions between the colonies and the British had been brewing for many years. The British passed many laws and taxes that colonists believed restricted their freedom and considered a hardship. Taxes on tea, sugar, paper, and other goods cost them economically.

The colonies had no real representation in Parliament, the British legislative body. Thus, "No Taxation Without Representation" became a popular

This illustration depicts the famous Boston Tea Party protest of December 16, 1773, when colonial activists protested British taxation by dumping tea into Boston Harbor.

revolutionary slogan and battle cry. Colonial leaders and citizens had other complaints about the British. In response to protests and other unrest, British troops were deployed. The British also passed laws forcing colonists to put up British soldiers in their homes and to provide them supplies out of their own pockets.

The colonists responded with several kinds of protest. One tactic they used was a boycott of imported British goods. They made their own similar products. But the thing that got the attention of the British the most was direct action—people gathering to voice their disapproval and anger in the streets.

THE FIRST AMENDMENT

The victorious Americans created their own government and adopted the United States Constitution as the law of the land in 1789. Ten amendments that guaranteed rights to the people themselves were added, or appended. This was the Bill of Rights. In addition to the freedoms of religion, the press, and to petition the government, the First Amendment guarantees freedom of speech and freedom of assembly. This makes the First Amendment the legal basis for all laws governing speech, protest, and political gatherings. It also makes it the basis for all challenges to laws that restrict these essential rights.

Not all protests or public gatherings are unconditionally guaranteed by the First Amendment. This includes the kind of speech that people use during demonstrations, protests, marches, or similar actions. The inclusion of this amendment guarantees—at least in theory—that ideas of all kinds would flourish. Most important, unpopular ones should ideally be protected by the force of law. The exact text of the First Amendment reads as follows:

> Congress shall make no law respecting an establishment of religion, or prohibiting the free exercise thereof; or abridging the freedom of speech, or of the press; or the right of the people peaceably to assemble, and to petition the government for a redress of grievances.

One of the most famous protests of the era became known as the Boston Tea Party. Many colonists were angry about a recent British law called the Tea Act. It allowed the British East India Company to sell its tea in the colonies at reduced prices, giving the British an unfair advantage and monopoly over the market. On December 16, 1773, a group of protesters known as the Sons of Liberty went into action. Some of the Sons of Liberty were famous anti-British figures, like Paul Revere. That night, they snuck aboard ships in Boston Harbor and destroyed about 46 tons (42 tonnes) of tea by dumping it overboard. Some were dressed in Native American costumes, partly to disguise themselves and partly as a signal of their loyalty to the New World over Britain. It was one instance in a long history of Americans using costumes to make statements during protests.

TRUE BELIEVERS: ABOLITION AND SUFFRAGE

Protests have served to publicize moral causes and to rally supporters to the movements surrounding them. Black freedmen and women joined with Quakers and other whites who opposed slavery to form the abolitionist movement in the nineteenth century. Their main goal was the abolition of slavery as an institution. They sent petitions with thousands of signatures to Congress and made newsletters to spread the word. Most important, abolitionists held public meetings and conferences, and made many speeches in public spaces

like squares. The movement was a major force in con-
vincing many Americans, especially northerners, that
slavery should be outlawed and blacks given full citi-
zenship and rights.

The fight for suffrage, or the right to vote, for women
in the late nineteenth and early twentieth centuries
marked one of the most important political victories and
milestones of the era. The eventual victory showed that
although protest might not yield immediate results, a
movement could build momentum over time. Some of
the techniques of suffragists included civil disobedience. For example, suffragist leader Susan B. Anthony
tried to vote during an 1872 election and was later arrested for it. Anthony used the resulting trial as a public
forum to fight even harder for the movement.

One major national suffragist protest in Washington,
DC, on March 3, 1913, brought out eight thousand
marchers. It featured musical groups, horse-mounted
brigades, and twenty floats. But the marchers faced
violence from onlookers, including many men in town for
the following day's presidential inauguration of Woodrow
Wilson. More than one hundred women were hospitalized
after being tripped, jostled, or otherwise attacked. But the
activists used it to turn public opinion to their cause. The
negative fallout was amplified in news stories, and the police superintendent of DC, blamed for police inaction that
allowed the attacks to go on, was even fired.

Others waged long-term actions. A group called the
Silent Sentinels began an ongoing protest in front of the
White House in Washington, DC, on January 10, 1917.
Many of them were abused by the authorities during the

This archival photo shows a band accompanying a parade of pro-testing suffragettes near the Capitol building in Washington, DC, one of many demonstrations of its kind during the early twentieth century.

picketing. In June, the DC police chief began ordering arrests of the women. At first, they were just three-day sentences for "obstructing traffic," a common and often trumped-up pretense. Looking back, most of the arrests were illegal, since they violated their rights to protest and public assembly.

However, many of the women were sentenced to sixty-day terms in jail. In jail some went on a hunger strike, refusing food while imprisoned. Others were put in solitary confinement. On November 14, a group of thirty-three returning protesters were savagely beaten by the guards upon their arrival at jail, including

CIVIL RIGHTS AND CIVIL DISOBEDIENCE

There are few protest movements that capture the imagination of Americans like the civil rights movement of the middle twentieth century. It included clergy and other people of faith, activist groups like the National Association for the Advancement of Colored People (NAACP), and student organizations like the Student Nonviolent Coordinating Committee (SNCC). These groups protested unfairly segregated facilities and racist Jim Crow laws. They borrowed tactics from other movements, like the successful Indian independence movement headed by Mahatma Gandhi years earlier.

Martin Luther King Jr. helped organize a series of marches for voting rights from Selma to Montgomery, both in Alabama, in 1965. They were inspired partly by similar actions of Gandhi's. Earlier activists staged sit-ins to protest segregated lunch counters and other segregated businesses in the late 1950s throughout the American South. These kinds of protests intentionally ignored the laws and authorities of the areas where they were staged. In fact, that was their whole point. They felt it was not only their right but their duty to challenge these unjust laws.

Other bold and often dangerous protest actions were the Freedom Rides held in 1961 and after. SNCC, the Congress of Racial Equality (CORE), and other groups recruited mostly young people of color to ride Southern segregated bus routes. Many of these actions were interrupted by white mobs at bus stations and along bus routes. They attacked and beat the activists. Local police often ignored, encouraged, or actively participated in attacking the Freedom Riders.

The March on Washington for Jobs and Freedom on August 28, 1963, was one of the most important events of the civil rights movement.

a seventy-three-year-old. The resulting news stories turned even more people against the police, and support for suffrage grew. All their efforts would yield victory in 1921, when the Nineteenth Amendment to the Constitution guaranteed women the right to vote.

WHAT HAS PROTEST ACCOMPLISHED?

Protests make some people feel uncomfortable. They attract attention to causes that otherwise may be ignored. Petitions and gradual change via voting and legislation work, too. But direct action can add pressure on top of more traditional routes to change. People protesting and voicing their opinions changed American society and history. The antiwar movement, especially on college campuses, helped end America's participation in the Vietnam War of the 1960s and 1970s. Civil rights activism undoubtedly forced politicians like President Lyndon B. Johnson to pass important legislation, including the Civil Rights Act of 1964. It outlawed discrimination based on race, religion, sex, nationality, or color. Protest movements of all kinds have had permanent, ongoing impacts on politics and society.

LEARNING FROM THE PAST

Young students of history and civics, especially protest, can trace how modern movements owe so much to earlier ones that fought social ills like slavery, sexism, anti-immigrant sentiment, and homophobia. The protests we see in the streets, on television, on social media, on college campuses, and even in high schools are part of a long tradition of dissent and social justice campaigning. Modern youth should feel especially empowered because they grew up with digital and social media network tools that have proven especially effective in advancing their causes. History also teaches them that they aren't powerless. Many important movements were filled with regular people, just like them, who cared deeply about things. It was the people who put their bodies in the streets who made things happen, and not just the famous leaders of movements often celebrated in history books and films.

OCCUPY WALL STREET, BLACK LIVES MATTER, AND MODERN PROTEST

The Tea Party protest movement rose in opposition to Barack Obama and Democratic policies, especially certain kinds of taxation, in 2009 and was named after the original Boston Tea Party. Despite controversy surrounding it—including claims by opponents that much of it had a racist component to it—Tea Party activism has achieved great success in getting many of its candidates in public office throughout all levels of government. It used social media and mainstream traditional media coverage in very effective ways, even if the activists and those who came to town halls to protest were often older Americans.

The Occupy movement protested corporate power over government and massive inequality in the United States. It began as an ongoing protest down in the

Protesters against economic inequality gathered in Manhattan's Zucotti Park near Wall Street on November 15, 2011, after earlier being ejected by police from the same location.

Wall Street area of Manhattan, at Zucotti Park. Activists moved into the park, and thousands visited over several weeks in the fall of 2011. Marches, rallies, and scuffles with the New York Police Department brought worldwide media attention. Its slogan was "We are the 99%," distinguishing regular people from the megarich who they said controlled society and government. Occupy protests spread to many cities. Many young people now involved in social justice campaigns say that visiting an Occupy encampment inspired them to continue activism.

The Black Lives Matter campaign, which formed in 2013, aims to end police brutality and killings of African Americans. One thing that BLM and Occupy had in common, and took advantage of, was the youth of many of their activists. They also used social media, including Twitter, Facebook, and other social media platforms, to great effect. In many ways, they set the standard for how these platforms could help organize protests. They also helped leaders and rank-and-file activists coordinate their street actions in real time. Successful, viral hashtags on Twitter and elsewhere spread the word far and wide.

MYTHS AND FACTS

MYTH: Freedom of speech means you can say whatever you want, whenever you want at any protest or other gathering.

FACT: There are specific laws covering what you can say, forbidding the provoking or inciting of violence, including speech that creates an atmosphere where others may likely retaliate against you. Even in a free society, no freedoms are absolute. Exchanging harsh words in person with others at a protest could cause trouble, including legal repercussions.

MYTH: Protesting is a simple, fun, and easy way to change the world for the better.

FACT: Activism, no matter what issue or cause you are fighting for, can often be a long, hard, and tedious process. More often than not, you will be disappointed. But it is often worth it if you believe in a cause that helps others and is done out of love and respect.

MYTH: People who protest are usually troublemakers who just want attention for themselves, or think they are entitled to everything they ask for.

FACT: It often takes a great deal of courage and conviction to come out and struggle nonviolently for a cause one believes in. Not everyone who protests does so for positive reasons, but many people who take to the streets do so because of their genuine and sincere beliefs.

CHAPTER TWO

KNOW YOUR RIGHTS, TAKE A STAND

Many people protest because they feel that other ways of making change are closed to them. Others use it as one tool in a bigger toolkit of tactics. There are many ways of expressing opposition to something. Some are more passive, others more militant. There may always be people who react negatively, no matter how passive or nonviolent the protest.

For example, there has been both enthusiastic support for and considerable backlash against Colin Kaepernick, the former quarterback of the San Francisco 49ers. In 2016, the star player began kneeling during the playing of the national anthem before each game to protest police killings of black Americans and racial injustice in America generally. National Football League (NFL) fans, sports writers and pundits, and even President Donald Trump attacked Kaepernick and other athletes for expressing their opinion with this seemingly moderate, innocuous protest. Kaepernick remained unsigned for the 2017 season. Many of his supporters say this was direct payback and launched an NFL boycott via Twitter and other platforms to stand

Colin Kaepernick took a knee during the national anthem at football games in protest of police violence against African Americans.

with him and other athletes.

Kaepernick's protest was a symbolic one. Protest takes many forms, however, and examining these can help us really get a sense of the kinds of actions that may be effective in achieving concrete goals.

PUBLIC ASSEMBLY AND FREE ASSOCIATION

The right to public assembly and protest are closely connected. People often use these terms interchangeably. Public assembly rights derive from the First Amendment's wording: " . . . the right of the people peaceably to assemble, and to petition the government for a redress of grievances." One can take this to mean that people can hold meetings in public (and private) for any reason and invite whomever they please. Another right that ties in here is freedom of association. For example, imagine a town government is planning to demolish a publicly owned building or build a disruptive pipeline, road, or other project. It will perhaps create a lot of traffic, noise, or even pollute the local environment. People who are affected, and those who support them, have the right to gather publicly to express their displeasure about it. The police and other authorities need to maintain order, certainly, but they cannot ban protests or gatherings like this, at least theoretically.

This right applies to all groups, no matter their religious or political beliefs. Christians, Muslims, and Jews all have this right, But so do people whose views or faith might make others uncomfortable or are unfamiliar to others, such as members of the Church of Satan, Scientologists, or Wiccans. If, for example, a Wiccan wanted to start a student group or hold a public question-and-answer session in the park, local authorities could not deny them a permit on the basis of their beliefs. Taking further guidance from the First Amendment, that student would then also have the right to organize actions to protest if that permit is denied.

FORWARD, MARCH!

Constitutionally, people can express themselves via protest in many public areas. These include streets, sidewalks, parks, public squares, and most public government buildings.

Protesters or those witnessing the action have the right to record the event, or take pictures of it. Police or other authorities have no right to confiscate a camera or other private property without a warrant or reasonable

On September 22, 2014, these climate change activists did a sit-in on Broadway, obstructing traffic in downtown Manhattan as part of an action called Flood Wall Street.

suspicion that there is illegal activity occurring. Anyone planning to attend a protest and/or take pictures or video footage should carefully research the local laws for their city, state, or federal statutes.

A rally in a particular place might need a permit. The stationary, or unmoving, protest could turn into a moving one, like a march. Under most circumstances, a march can go pretty much anywhere as long as it does not block off the sidewalk to those who need to access it or block traffic in the street itself. Rallies can be effective because they can attract the attention of passersby or other community members. A student rally, for example, would ideally occur near some school building or facility, or any other spot where students might naturally gather.

Marches can expose others to protesters' ideas or demands because they may get the attention from those who might not otherwise encounter them. Students protesting a campus policy might march to an administrative meeting or offices. They might also march by the house of a school president or principal to air grievances. Depending on their goals, they should try to keep certain kinds of marches minimally disruptive to innocent bystanders, local residents, or others who deserve respect and privacy.

CIVIL DISOBEDIENCE: REFUSE AND RESIST

Rallies and marches are just one tool groups use to advance an agenda or raise awareness. Some groups endorse civil disobedience and more militant actions. With civil disobedience, the whole point is to protest something unjust by breaking some rule or regulation, or the law itself. Most people regard nonviolence as essential to civil disobedience. Using it brings attention and sympathy to issues and causes.

For instance, in 2017, Republican politicians and President Donald Trump announced new legislation to dismantle and repeal the Affordable Care Act (ACA, often known as Obamacare) covering health insurance. Many people protested multiple repeal attempts. One of the most powerful and effective actions was organized by ADAPT, which stands for Americans Disabled Attendant Programs Today. Dozens of wheelchair-bound and otherwise disabled activists, including senior citizens, occupied congressional offices. The sight of them being carried out of government buildings by police was a great tool to bring people to their cause. Some shouted, "Don't touch Medicaid, save our liberty," according to CNN. Police handled some demonstrators roughly. This only made people even more sympathetic. On several occasions throughout 2017, such actions helped defeat repeated attempts at repealing the law.

A wheelchair-bound activist joined others to express outrage at US lawmakers' efforts to repeal and replace the Affordable Care Act in February 2017 during a protest in Los Angeles.

Like the lunch counter sit-ins of the civil rights era, the aim was to stir the public conscience. Civil disobedience can include trespassing, refusing to disperse, disturbing the peace, and other minor charges. Still, activists engaging in such actions should be ready for arrest and to possibly spend one or more nights in prison before they are bailed out or released.

THE PICKET LINE

Another form of protest is picketing. Union members and activists have used the picket line for a long time.

Members of Ironworkers Local 361 picketed a work site at Brooklyn's Pratt Institute in March 2009, their protest made more colorful by the presence of a large, inflatable rat.

When people walk off the job to protest poor wages or bad conditions, some or all employees picket outside the workplace. They may do so partly to discourage other workers from entering it. Workers who cross a picket line may be jeered and called the insulting term "scab." Ide-

A RESURGENCE OF LABOR—AND PROTEST

The largest workers' strike of recent memory was a forty-five-day picket of Verizon by nearly forty thousand employees that lasted from April to May 2016. With record profits in recent years, the company was criticized by the Communication Workers of America (CWA), which called the strike to protest job losses to outsourcing. After the strike, Verizon reversed several decisions, adding jobs and improving wages and benefits. "Because we fought together as a union, my kids will be able to see me at night," call center employee Christina Martin told the CWA's website newsletter.

In addition, many different groups organized actions. Many of these have united under the "Fight for $15" umbrella. The movement arose from fast-food workers throughout the nation risking their jobs with walkouts and short strikes to force the issue with their employers and local governments. Their successes in helping passage of a $15 minimum wage in many cities and towns have astounded many people who thought the labor movement was continuing to decline. Cities like Los Angeles, San Francisco, Emeryville, and Mountain View in California, Seattle, Washington, Pittsburgh, Pennsylvania, and many others have approved wage raises.

ally, a picket should be nonviolent, even if it is boisterous and theatrical. In New York City and other cities, union members in the construction trades sometimes picket nonunion work sites. Often, they bring a giant inflatable rat, which workers have sometimes nicknamed "Scabby."

In some cases, picketers want to bring attention to an issue and do it in plain view and earshot of those with whom they have grievances. For example, in 1988, director Martin Scorsese, himself a Catholic, released his controversial film *The Last Temptation of Christ*. Many religious groups, including Catholics, staged pickets of cinemas playing the film. Antiabortion activists have been known to frequently picket women's health clinics. Some are respectful, but others have been condemned for intimidating women, whether they are seeking abortions or merely gynecological care.

SYMBOLS, SYMBOLIC PROTESTS, AND VISUAL EXPRESSION

If you have ever seen a protest live or on television, or been involved with one yourself, you know that protesters often carry signs. Protests gain their strength from many rallying or marching for a common goal. Signs, especially homemade ones, allow individuals to express themselves in specific and often fun and uniquely creative ways. The same is true for T-shirts, buttons, and other visual media. Potent symbols include the American flag, the peace sign, and a clenched black fist (a frequent symbol of anti-racist activism, black power, and resistance in general).

Costumes can be both fun and effective in activism. Here, food safety protesters march in favor of aggressively regulating the cloning of cows and other livestock.

Another way people use symbolic imagery is by using costumes, much like people on floats during a parade. One popular choice for many people is to wear exaggerated, caricatured masks or costumes of political leaders. Costumes might also include using temporary tattoos or face or body paint to pointed effect.

For example, those protesting Democratic nominee Hillary Clinton during the 2016 campaign sometimes wore masks or printed cut outs of her face, complete with a striped prisoner uniform. This was a way to call her a criminal who deserved imprisonment. Anti-Obama protesters sometimes made costumes of the president. Some of these had disturbing, inappropriate, and even racist connotations. Nevertheless, while they may have provoked anger among many onlookers, they were protected as free speech. The same is true of those who choose to wear costumes or masks spoofing the distinctive appearance of President Donald Trump.

Even very provocative and racist symbols—like the Nazi swastika denoting support of Nazi Germany or racist caricatures of blacks, Jews, Muslims, or others—have generally been upheld as constitutional and legal over the years. The same is true for racist hand gestures, including the Roman salute, which was appropriated by the German Nazis as the "Sieg Heil" salute—translated as "Hail victory!" and interpreted as support for Naziism or Nazi-like policies and goals. The Confederate flag, also adopted by many white nationalist groups, including the Ku Klux Klan, is defended as a symbol of Southern heritage by many. Many other Americans, especially blacks, recognize it as a potent and hurtful symbol of the era of slavery and black disenfranchisement. In the context of protesting, it is often used to convey a certain worldview.

If you attend a protest, think long and hard about using symbols or imagery that may be controversial. It may be effective in the short term, but it can hurt the cause in the greater scheme of things. Be sure not to intentionally or even accidentally use images that disparage other people's ethnicity, religion, disabilities, sexual orientation or identity, or similar qualities. Concentrate on the policies or actions of the government or issue that is being protested.

Above all, make sure that no sign slogans or imagery may be construed as directly threatening anyone. Making threats against public figures, especially implying that you will harm them, or take their life, is not just dangerous and distasteful, but illegal. Outside of legitimate self-defense, violence can also be highly counterproductive, It can also land you in jail, possibly for a long time, depending on the consequences of your actions in the heat of the moment.

CHAPTER THREE

THE LIMITS OF PROTEST

There are other dos and don'ts when it comes to protesting and gathering. Taking a look at these boundaries can especially help younger people who are looking to get involved in their schools and communities, and in the world at large. They can learn from the mistakes of others and examine the historical record to see what has worked.

In theory, free speech itself, along with protests and public assembly, is broadly defined and protected. But in reality, there are many rules and regulations surrounding the exercise of these rights. Many of these rules are legitimate and commonsense ones put in place to protect communities, institutions, and people, and maintain public order.

PERMITS: TIME, PLACE, AND MANNER

According to the American Civil Liberties Union (ACLU), permits are usually not required for free speech activities. But certain types of events do require them. As explained on the "Know Your Rights: What to Do If Your Rights Are Violated at a Demonstration or Protest" page of the ACLU's website, these might include: "a march or parade that does not stay on the sidewalk, and other events that require blocking traffic or street closure"; "a large rally requiring the use of sound amplifying devices [like microphones, megaphones, speakers, and other equipment]; and rallies "at certain designated parks or plazas."

Cities, towns, and other jurisdictions often decide on who will be able to protest or gather in a particular place and time. This is done via approving permits. The organization or groups of organizations, or people lead-

A ten-year-old boy was among a group of Black Lives Matter demonstrators gathered outside a Baltimore Police Department (BPD) station on April 22, 2015, to protest the death of Freddie Gray.

ing the action are required to apply for these according to local laws. To get the permits, they must often agree to certain rules.

Additionally, the ACLU points out that the First Amendment prohibits restrictions on permits and gatherings based on the content of speech. This applies also to the assumed political beliefs or aims of the groups trying to gather. "Police and government officials are allowed to place certain nondiscriminatory and narrowly 'time, place, and manner' restrictions on the exercise of First Amendment rights," declares the ACLU's "Know Your Rights" webpage. "Any such restrictions must apply to all speech regardless of its point of view."

Naturally, some restrictions might be harsh or unfair. Others may be fair in theory but may be unevenly applied. Activists, especially for controversial and unpopular causes, often complain of discriminatory treatment. Even groups like the Ku Klux Klan, despite their often hateful views, are entitled under the law to public forums for their speech. Communities, government officials, or police departments may go out of their way to restrict (fairly or unfairly) gatherings that might attract people who they predict will be violent or destructive.

GOING THROUGH THE PERMIT PROCESS

Imagine you belong to a community-based organization with some classmates, neighbors, and community members. You decide to protest your town's treatment of its homeless population or other issue. What might be some of the things one has to do to get a rally and march off the ground?

Many municipalities (cities, towns) have different rules, but they generally resemble each other. First, the group should gather the information they need to give to the government or authority dispensing the permit. There should be a realistic estimate of the number of people expected. The site of the rally should be detailed—for example, with an address. If the rally includes or is a march, the exact expected route should be indicated. The exact date, time, and duration of the event needs to be detailed. Make sure to stick to these, too.

Occupy Wall Street protesters faced off against New York Police Department officers across a barricade in November 2011. Controversy arose over both police and activists' behavior.

You may need to call or visit the appropriate office weeks ahead. Organizers need to do their research, too. Do not expect to get a permit for a rally in a business district protesting homeless policy in late December if you know that there is always a holiday bazaar or marketplace there every year, for example.

Be prepared to pay a fee of some kind. Your money may help contribute to trash cleanup after an event. A security deposit might be required, if guards or other security measures have to be paid for by a town or other entity, such as a university. Money may go to overtime pay for local police. A "Defend the Homeless" march will not likely incur big fees up front. There is also a chance that one's town might allow a waiver (the ability to ignore the fee) for groups that simply can't afford it.

PERMIT: DENIED!

What should an organizer or group do if a permit is denied? It all depends on what the reasons were, of course. But, say, for instance, that your town's government tried to charge your group $25,000, which it claimed would go to police overtime or a variety of other charges. The ACLU states, "If the costs are greater because an event is controversial (or a hostile crowd is expected)—such as requiring a large insurance policy—then the courts will not permit it." Of course, the town may deny the permit or insist on the onerous, or extremely demanding, fee.

There may be other reasons a permit is denied. A transparent (open) government will provide its reasons, but it may not legally be required to. In the case of the homeless protest, it may be because the city has an interest or desire not to have its laws challenged. One way to hold a government's feet to the fire, so to speak, is to research recent and similar rallies or actions. Check government records or archives, go online, or even contact organizers directly. Did other groups get permission for their events? Chances are if they had a smooth ride, it may be your group that has been singled out.

An activist group run on a shoestring budget may not be able to afford legal redress in court. It helps if there is a lawyer involved on the activists' side. A firm

Occupy protesters listen to attorney Samuel Cohen provide information on pro bono legal aid on behalf of activists arrested or prosecuted during the 2011 protests in downtown Manhattan.

could take up the group's cause pro bono, for free. Some do so and specialize in activist causes.

The most famous legal organization that handles such cases is the ACLU. Getting groups through the legal hoops of protest permits is one of its specialties. Nearly every state has an ACLU affiliate, and many have several, perhaps even near you. It is worthwhile to contact the ACLU if there is enough time for it to act on a group's behalf.

FIGHTING WORDS

In 1940, Walter Chaplinsky, a street preacher and Jehovah's Witness, was arrested by a town marshal, accused of calling him a "God-damned racketeer" and a "a damned fascist." The court ruled against him, declaring that the First Amendment did not protect "fighting words"—speech that would cause, in the words of Justice Frank Murphy, "those which by their very utterance inflict injury or tend to incite an immediate breach of the peace."

Tensions at protests can boil over quickly into physical violence. For example, some Unite the Right right-wing demonstrators in Charlottesville in August 2017 were physically violent. But it remains debatable whether some of their words may not have been criminal, too. Vox writer Alexia Campbell noted, "While the generic antisemitic and anti-immigrant rants didn't rise to fighting words," demonstrators may have crossed the line when they used common and offensive slurs for African Americans and gays, because "they are slurs directed at certain individuals that would lead a reasonable person to retaliate."

However, since the Chaplinksy decision, justices of the Supreme Court have tended to narrow their definition of fighting words. Fearing that they might restrict speech unnecessarily, they have tried to subject an insult to a three-part test. First, the language must be insulting. Second, the words must be said more or less face to face. Third, the words must be likely to provoke retaliation. On the other hand, lower courts have been more likely to rule against people who use aggressive or threatening insults, especially ones with a racial component.

Fighting words relate to an important precedent that has guided the Supreme Court on and off when it comes to regulating protest: "clear and present danger." In 1919,

LEAFLETING AND OTHER PROTEST SPEECH

Even in this digital age, leafleting—handing out printed materials that promote a cause or inform the public about injustices or alert them about protest actions—is still a very popular form of speech. You can approach people on public streets and sidewalks with newsletters or leaflets and also ask them to sign petitions or donate money to your cause. Tables where you leave your literature for others to look through are also allowed in most public places, but these may require permits in many areas. Do not block the sidewalk or block entrances to buildings or businesses, or otherwise prevent others from going about their private and public business in any way.

the Supreme Court ruled against a protester speaking against the military draft during World War I. In the case *Schenck v. United States*, Justice Oliver Wendell Holmes Jr. said that the man's action was like "shouting fire in a crowded theater." This meant that actions that would probably cause violence or endanger society in some way could be barred. Ever since, people have been fighting over the vague meaning of "clear and present." Many believe that government officials usually have too wide a definition and use it to suppress unpopular speech.

DEALING WITH POLICE

Tensions have flared up between many activists and police lately. Because of the nature of their issue, activists protesting police violence have seemed to have been particularly targeted and policed more heavily in the streets.

Police may have specific orders for any particular shift they work at a protest. This does not necessarily mean that every officer is fully informed on constitutional free speech rights. These may differ among jurisdictions. The laws also change, without many people even being aware of them, police and protesters alike. Generally, the ACLU, other nongovernmental organizations, and those who mentor and train activists advise newcomers to tread lightly when dealing with police. This is doubly true in the heat of the moment.

If a police officer acts aggressively or prevents your free movement, the ACLU advises: "It rarely does any

Riot police blocked counterprotesters from physical contact with far-right activists during a Boston "Free Speech" rally on August 19, 2017, a week after a violent showdown in Charlottesville, Virginia.

good to argue with a street patrol officer. Ask to talk to a supervisor and explain your position to him or her. Point out that you are not disrupting anyone else's activity and that the First Amendment protects your actions."

Disobeying orders to disperse can subject you to arrest. You may be handled roughly. Some protesters have won huge settlements after being injured by police during protests. But most people would prefer not to risk being arrested. Nobody wants to end up in the hospital or get seriously hurt. One can always complain later and file First Amendment violation charges against an individual police officer, or against a police department, a town, or a city.

10 GREAT QUESTIONS TO ASK AN ACTIVIST

1. How do you join an activist group?
2. Do you think there are any causes that shouldn't be allowed to protest or have a voice in a democracy?
3. How do you respond to criticism that some protests are too disruptive or inconvenient to others?
4. What other kinds of protest or activist tactics do you use in addition to showing up somewhere in person?
5. How do you prepare to deal with the police or other authorities?
6. How do you de-escalate situations that may become chaotic or violent?
7. In what ways can smartphones and social media help with on-the-ground organizing during protests and similar gatherings?
8. What was the event or situation that inspired you to protest for the first time?
9. How do you stay safe at protests?
10. Have you seen any positive outcomes in the real world arising out of protests you have engaged in?

CHAPTER FOUR

GETTING INVOLVED

In some ways, it has never been easier to get involved with a cause. Social media allows likeminded people, especially youth, to come together easily. If you had your heart set on it, you could probably start organizing an action today, just from your personal contacts.

However, many activists and scholars of social justice and civics are also troubled. Since the terrorist attacks on American soil on September 11, 2001, there have been ever increasing restrictions on protest and free speech by the government. These include constant surveillance by the government of Internet usage, phone calls and texts, and other communications, as exposed by ex-CIA whistleblower Edward Snowden. Both protesters and innocent journalists were caught up in police dragnets during the January 20, 2017, protests during the inauguration of Donald Trump. Several later faced harsh prison sentences for riot-related charges—even those who did not act violently but merely recorded the chaos.

The ability of social media to amplify not only some of the best impulses around activism, but some of the worst, has also made things complicated for young people thinking about advocating for change. However, these things should be seen by young people as things to push back against creatively.

WHAT'S YOUR ISSUE?

You probably already have a good idea what issues inspire or enrage you. You probably follow one or more causes, perhaps online. See what gets you upset, drives you to get involved, and out to a meeting—and, eventually, a protest, once you're ready. No matter

Protesters rallied in Las Vegas, Nevada, against the Trump administration's likely scrapping of the Deferred Action for Childhood Arrivals (DACA) program, which protects foreign-born youth from deportation.

where you are, there is likely a group that fits your needs and beliefs.

There are church- and other faith-based groups that protest to help the poor and needy. Organizations advocating for immigrants' rights or to help fight Islamophobia or antisemitism, such as the Muslim Public Affairs Council or the Anti-Defamation League (ADL), are also out there. Others fight for free speech rights, like the Foundation for Individual Rights in Education (FIRE). There are also many smaller, grassroots organizations that both work with and independently of bigger ones. Such groups exist in all communities. In fact, these are the ones that most need volunteers and donations. Donating your time and energy is perhaps even more valuable than financial assistance, especially if you have limited means.

FIRST AND NEXT STEPS

If you feel hesitant and need to ease in to social justice or other campaigns, one way to start is to find people to follow on Twitter, Tumblr, or other platforms. Check out their activity and visit the websites of groups you are interested in. You may dabble in or dip your toes in the waters by commenting on posts. Learn the ins and outs of the way people talk in activist spaces, and make sure to address people respectfully.

Educate yourself. Avoid pressuring others to educate you. Engage strangers politely to ask for articles and books to familiarize you with a particular cause or a group's struggles and efforts. Reputable organizations with many members will usually have thorough and extensive websites, with educational links, and plenty of literature discussing their philosophies, organization, and goals.

Of course, depending on the issue, direct action might need to happen now and not later. Imagine a local conservation group trying to save a nearby forest preserve: they might have to mobilize quickly. A sudden and unexpected action by local officials or other parties might force people's hand. In such cases, it is OK to ask a teacher, parent, family member, or other trusted adult if they might be interested in accompanying you.

A walkout—like this one by New York City high school students in February 2017 to protest US immigration policies—is one tactic that has proven popular with youth activists.

For certain events and actions, it may be required, especially if things may potentially get chaotic. Do your research by reading about similar actions that have happened recently. Newcomers might want to avoid possibly dangerous situations or ones with heavy and aggressive police presence, at least at first.

DOING YOUR PART

There is a first time for everything, including being new to an activist group. It should be relatively easy to figure out who is in charge, even when coming upon strangers with signs getting ready to protest. At a meeting, you need only listen and often members and officers will introduce themselves and talk about their roles.

Everyone has a job to do. Make clear to the organization what your skillset is. If you are computer savvy, you may be assigned to do web design or handle social media posts. First-timers might do more menial tasks, like stuffing envelopes for mailings, researching press clippings online, shopping for supplies, or cleaning up. Usually, many tasks will be shared among members. Jobs may switch weekly or from meeting to meeting.

STAYING SAFE (OFFLINE AND ONLINE)

Many groups of experienced activists hold meetups ahead of protests to train newcomers on the basics of how to march, who to avoid, how to stay safe around

Smartphones have made it ever easier for like-minded young activists to connect, strategize, and coordinate efforts to make concrete changes in their communities and society.

the police, and what to do if they themselves or others are somehow split up, hurt, or arrested. This is especially important nowadays, when tensions have increased between protesters and the authorities, including law enforcement agencies, whether local police forces or the Federal Bureau of Investigation (FBI), among others.

Be careful of what you post online. Stay respectful and clear headed. Crossing certain lines can get you suspended or banned from a social media network. You may even be investigated by the authorities if your words can be misinterpreted as threatening a public official, another person, or public order.

Also remain on high alert for strange individuals who may take advantage of people new to protest and activism. Some might even be undercover police, seeing who they can sweep up and provoke into criminal speech or actions. There has been much controversy over FBI stings and other police actions taken against people who were simply posting the "wrong" opinions online.

Others might simply be predators and not activists at all. Do not give out personal information to others online that you have not met in person. Even if you meet them in real life (IRL), it is vital to make sure people are who they say they are. Some online digging can easily establish who's who. For groups that have limited budgets and may not even have websites, ask others to double check for you that they are legitimate.

AVOID DOXXING (OR GETTING DOXXED)

Smartphone cameras are seemingly everywhere. Protests often attract media attention, too. Combined with social media, including Facebook groups, Twitter threads, and so much more, it is easier than ever to identify members of activist groups or protest attendees. It takes a few shorts steps online, and it is even quicker for those who pay for online search services. Some groups, including antifa-associated ones, make it part of their activism to doxx, or expose, the

Former pastor and blogger Shaun King, now a columnist for the *New York Daily News*, is one of a generation of new activist leaders who use social media activism to push for social justice causes.

identities of far-right activists, for example. Far-right groups do the same to antifa as well. Such activity can be both beneficial and problematic.

For instance, *Daily News* writer and Black Lives Matter supporter Shaun King made it a mission to identify several attackers who seriously beat Charlottesville counterprotester Deandre Harris. Using a video of the men striking Harris in a parking lot with flagpoles, he was able to use his many followers on Twitter to identify and help police arrest several of them.

BLACK LIVES MATTER: A NEW CIVIL RIGHTS MOVEMENT

Black Lives Matter, or BLM, grew from an online hashtag on social media—#BlackLivesMatter on Facebook, Twitter, and elsewhere—to a national and international movement opposing police violence and systemic racism in general. The original activists who invented the hashtag and popularized the movement were Alicia Garza, Patrisse Cullors, and Opal Tometi. They were expressing their rage and heartbreak at the July 2013 acquittal of George Zimmerman. Zimmerman was acquitted of second-degree murder and other charges after stalking African American teenager Trayvon Martin in Sanford, Florida, ultimately shooting and killing the teenager.

Their activism helped grow a larger movement around incidents like the Zimmerman case and the many shootings of unarmed black citizens by police nationwide. One of the first in-person actions organized by BLM was a protest responding to the August 2014 fatal police shooting of teenager Michael Brown in Ferguson, Missouri.

For many youth, BLM is the most wide-reaching and vocal group addressing the civil rights struggles of African Americans in a new era. It is decentralized. This means groups in many cities operate mostly independently of each other. Wherever a controversial police shooting occurred from 2014 onwards, BLM activists were likely to be on the scene, protesting police precincts, and using other tactics, like blocking public spaces, including highways.

BLM has also attracted controversy. Its critics say its tactics are disruptive and sometimes illegal, ignoring permits and other formalities. Some propolice groups claim

BLM is a hate group. But supporters and members active with BLM point out that they are simply demanding that police stop killing black people. They point out that if their protests were not disruptive enough, nobody would pay attention to a problem many want to ignore in the first place.

Other cases of mistaken identity have gotten people targeted for online pile-ons and harassment campaigns before people realized their mistake. Imagine, for example, if you are merely walking by a protest and you are mistakenly identified as part of it. Even people who are later found to be innocent can be "convicted" in the court of public opinion.

In addition, some activists and protesters may not want their involvement to be revealed to their employers, families, or other acquaintances. LGBTQ individuals, for example, may not have come out to their families. Meanwhile, their photos are plastered all over the media. A good rule of thumb if you are thinking of doxxing someone is usually, "Just because you can, doesn't mean you should." Take a step back and think about what you are doing.

Activist youth are advised to keep any and all accounts with personal information private. Police and other authorities are definitely out there watching. Even if photos and information online does not expose you to prosecution for anything—likely, you are not doing anything illegal—it can be used to undermine your cause or exert pressure on friends, family, and acquaintances.

FORMING YOUR OWN GROUP, AND JOINING WITH OTHERS

Groups of all sizes are eager for new, young, enthusiastic members. They also groom especially talented and sincere ones for higher posts in their organizations, including leadership positions. If you are lucky enough to bond with an older person, pick his or her brains and gain all the experience you can. Having such a mentor is as great as reading dozens of books.

If you get some activism under your belt, you may be ready to help others get into it. Forming your own group can be fantastic. Others may not be able to address a

Hundreds of New York City college and high school youth took to the streets on April 29, 2015, to protest the death of Baltimore resident Freddie Gray.

particular issue like you can. You may have different opinions on it than others you have worked under before. This does not mean that you cannot join forces with others with whom you may disagree on minor points. Many groups unite in a common front to protest when the time comes.

JUST THE BEGINNING

Activism can become a job or take up all one's time outside of school or work. It can be a very positive force in one's life. The world can seem like a cold, unforgiving place. Marching in solidarity for a cause can make you feel part of something and less alone. Realize, however, that it is only part of the work activists do. When they're not in the streets, activists are doing equally important but less exciting work: filing petitions, making phone calls to officials and politicians, volunteering with organizations that help others, pushing others to support legislation, and much more.

It is also important to take a break sometimes. Don't feel you have to march all the time and go to every event. Getting burned out is a major reason some people stop being active. Everyone needs time to recharge, pursue other hobbies, and see friends, family, and loved ones. They also need time away from politics to keep their relationships with those who may not agree with them.

GLOSSARY

abolitionist A person who fought actively to end the institution of slavery.

action A general term for any demonstration, rally, march, sit-in, or other form of protest.

amplify To increase the volume of something, especially sound, or to help spread news or an idea.

boisterous Energetic, cheerful, or loud.

civil liberties Rights that belong to individuals who theoretically cannot or should not be taken away by the government.

decentralized Refers to groups that operate independently but are essentially fighting for the same goals.

direct action The use of in-person tactics, like strikes, demonstrations, or other public protests.

disparage To insult or regard as being lesser or worthless.

dissent Disagreeing with ideas or policies, especially those of the government.

doxxing Revealing someone's private information or identity online, usually with the intent of directing harassment at the individual or otherwise getting the individual in trouble.

fighting words Speech, including hateful slurs, that is designed to provoke an aggressive response in others.

grassroots Refers to organizations and actions that are run by regular people who feel strongly about an issue.

grievance Complaint of unfair treatment against the government or other institution.

Jim Crow A term describing a wide-ranging set of discriminatory laws throughout many states and communities in the United States that denied African Americans civil and political rights from the late nineteenth century through the 1960s and 1970s.

militant Describes activism and protest that is more aggressive and confrontational, and that may or may not favor violence as a tactic.

picketing Showing up outside a place to protest.

pro bono Short for *pro bono publico* (Latin for "for the public good"), refers to legal work done for free as a public service.

social justice The fight for causes that seek equal treatment and opportunity for all people under the law and within society generally.

suffragist A person who fought for voting rights, especially for women.

transparent Refers to open and visible government activity, which helps people hold their officials responsible for their actions.

utterance Something that is spoken, whether a word, speech, or sound.

FOR MORE INFORMATION

American Civil Liberties Union
125 Broad Street, 18th Floor
New York, NY 10004
(212) 549-2500
Website: https://www.aclu.org
Facebook: @aclu.nationwide
Twitter: @aclu
YouTube: @acluvideos
The ACLU works to preserve civil liberties through lobbying and legal action via both in national headquarters and affiliates in more than fifty states and has been responsible for some of the most important civil liberties victories in US courts since its founding in 1920.

Canadian Civil Liberties Association
90 Eglinton Avenue East, Suite 900
Toronto ON M42 2Y3
Canada
(416) 363-0321
Website: https://ccla.org
Facebook and Twitter: @cancivlib
Founded in 1964, the Canadian Civil Liberties Association is an independent, national, nongovernmental organization working via the courts, legislation, and the educational system, and on the streets to defend the rights and freedoms of Canadians.

Direct Action & Resource Training Center (DART)
9401 Biscayne Boulevard, Suite 215
Miami Shores, FL 33138
(305) 576-8020
Website: http://www.thedartcenter.org
DART is a national network of twenty-two affiliated
    grassroots, nonprofit, religious congregation-based
    community organizations across eight states that
    provides training on direct action to community or-
    ganizers and activists.

Equitas
666 Sherbrooke Street West, Suite 1100
Montreal, QC H3A 1E7
Canada
(514) 954-0382
Website: https://equitas.org
Facebook: @Equitas
Twitter: @equitasintl
YouTube: @EquitasHRE
Equitas is one of Canada's most recognized and active
    human rights education organizations, working for
    equality, social justice, and other aims through edu-
    cational programs and training.

Foundation for Individual Rights in Education (FIRE)
510 Walnut Street, Suite 1250
Philadelphia, PA 19106
(215) 717-FIRE (3473)
Email: fire@thefire.org

Website: https://www.thefire.org

Twitter, Facebook, and YouTube: @theFireOrg

FIRE is a nonprofit that concentrates on defending civil liberties, especially academic freedom, on campuses throughout America, including those of both students and faculty.

Resource Center for Nonviolence

612 Ocean Street

Santa Cruz, CA 95060

(831) 423-1626

Email: rcnvinfo@gmail.com

Website: http://rcnv.org

Facebook: @rcnvsc

Twitter: @RCNV1

Founded in 1976, the Resource Center for Nonviolence is a peace and justice organization that promotes nonviolent social change, including partnerships nationwide, throughout Latin America and the Middle East, and elsewhere.

FOR FURTHER READING

Aretha, David. *The Story of the Selma Voting Rights Marches in Photographs*. Berkeley Heights, NJ: Enslow Publishers, 2014.

Braun, Eric. *Taking Action for Civil and Political Rights*. Minneapolis, MN: Lerner Publications, 2017.

Jack, Zachary Michael. *March of the Suffragettes: Rosalie Gardiner Jones and the March for Voting Rights*. Boston, MA: Zest, 2016.

Kimmel, Allison Crotzer. *The Montgomery Bus Boycott*. North Mankato, MN: Capstone Press, 2015.

Lusted, Marcia Amidon, and Gerald J. Thain. *Tinker v. Des Moines: The Right to Protest in Schools*. Minneapolis, MN: ABDO Publishing, 2013.

Pauly, Robert J. *Speech, Media, and Protest*. Broomall, PA: Mason Crest, 2017.

Schwartz, Heather E. *The March on Washington: A Primary Source Exploration of the Pivotal Protest*. North Mankato, MN: Capstone Press, 2015.

Smith-Lera, Danielle. *Black Power Salute: How a Photograph Captured a Political Protest*. North Mankato, MN: Compass Point Books, 2017.

Spence, Kelly. *Martin Luther King Jr. and Peaceful Protest*. New York, NY: Cavendish Square, 2017.

Terp, Gail, and William Powell Jones. *Nonviolent Resistance in the Civil Rights Movement*. Minneapolis, MN: Core Library/ABDO Publishing, 2016.

BIBLIOGRAPHY

American Civil Liberties Union. "Know Your Rights: Demonstrations and Protests." Retrieved September 23, 2017. https://www.aclu.org/sites/default/files /field_pdf_file/kyr_protests.pdf.

American Civil Liberties Union. "Rights of Protesters." Retrieved September 21, 2017. https://www.aclu .org/issues/free-speech/rights-protesters.

Atlanta Black Star."ACLU Sues St. Louis Over Treatment of Protesters." September 22, 2017. http:// atlantablackstar.com/2017/09/22/aclu-sues-st-louis -treatment-protesters.

Baptiste, Nathalie. "Origins of a Movement." *The Nation*, February 9, 2017. https://www.thenation.com /article/origins-of-a-movement.

Bill of Rights Institute. "Freedom of Speech: General." Retrieved September 17, 2017. http://www .billofrightsinstitute.org/educate/educator-resources /landmark-cases/freedom-of-speech-general.

Blake, Riley. "An NYU Student's Guide to Protesters' Rights." *Washington Square News*, April 24, 2017. https://www.nyunews.com/2017/04/24/an-nyu -students-guide-to-protesters-rights.

Campbell, Alexia Fernández. "Some Racist, Homophobic Chants in Charlottesville May Not Be Protected Under 1st Amendment." Vox.com, August 15, 2017. https://www.vox.com/policy-and-politics/2017/8/15 /16144058/charlottesville-free-speech.

Communication Workers of America. "Big Gains for
    Striking Verizon Workers in New Agreement." Press
    release, May 29, 2016. https://www.cwa-union.org
    /news/releases/big-gains-for-striking-verizon
    -workers-in-new-agreement.
Library of Congress. "Right to Peaceful Assembly: Unit-
    ed States." Retrieved September 20, 2017. https://
    www.loc.gov/law/help/peaceful-assembly/us.php.
Meyer, David S. *The Politics of Protest: Social Move-
    ments in America*. 2nd ed. New York, NY: Oxford
    University Press, 2014.
The Rutherford Institute. "Constitutional Corner." Re-
    trieved September 20, 2017. https://www.rutherford
    .org/constitutional_corner.
Smith, David, and Luc Torres. "Timeline: A History of
    Free Speech." *Guardian*, February 5, 2006. https://
    www.theguardian.com/media/2006/feb/05/religion
    .news.
Terruso, Julia. "Camden Students Walk Out to Protest
    Layoffs." *Inquirer*, May 15, 2014. http://www.philly
    .com/philly/news/new_jersey/20140515_Camden
    _students_walk_out_to_protest_layoffs.html.

INDEX

ABOUT THE AUTHOR

Philip Wolny is a writer and editor from Queens, New York. He has written about constitutional rights, politics, history, and culture for Rosen Publishing, including *Gun Rights: Interpreting the Constitution*, *Colonialism: A Primary Source Analysis*, and *Muslims Around the World Today*. He has also written many instructional and self-help books for young adults.

PHOTO CREDITS

Cover Portland Press Herald/Getty Images; pp. 5, 28–29, 32 Chip Somodevilla/Getty Images; pp. 7, 19, 31, 42 (background) Sheila Fitzgerald/Shutterstock .com; p. 8 MPI/Archive Photos/Getty Images; p. 12 Bettmann/Getty Images; p. 14 Consolidated News Pictures/Hulton Archive/Getty Images; p. 16 Michael Nagle/Getty Images; p. 20 Michael Zagaris/Getty Images; p. 22 Bryan Thomas/Getty Images; pp. 24, 52 Anadolu Agency/Getty Images; pp. 25, 36, 49 © AP Images; p. 34 Andrew Burton/Getty Images; pp. 40, 45 Spencer Platt/Getty Images; p. 43 Ethan Miller/Getty Images; p. 47 SpeedKingz/Shutterstock.com.

Design: Michael Moy; Layout: Ellina Litmanovich; Editor: Amelie von Zumbusch; Photo Researcher: Karen Huang